The Light Around Us

About the Author

Candela Wicke is a gemmologist and coloured-light therapist based in the UK.

This thrilling work combination has recently taken her on many exciting journeys, and she is looking forward to more opportunities to roam the globe and share the wonder of light with others.

THE LIGHT AROUND US

Candela Wicke

Copyright © 2018 Candela Wicke

The moral right of the author has been asserted.

Apart from any fair dealing for the purposes of research or private study, or criticism or review, as permitted under the Copyright, Designs and Patents Act 1988, this publication may only be reproduced, stored or transmitted, in any form or by any means, with the prior permission in writing of the publishers, or in the case of reprographic reproduction in accordance with the terms of licences issued by the Copyright Licensing Agency. Enquiries concerning reproduction outside those terms should be sent to the publishers.

Matador
9 Priory Business Park,
Wistow Road, Kibworth Beauchamp,
Leicestershire. LE8 0RX
Tel: 0116 279 2299
Email: books@troubador.co.uk
Web: www.troubador.co.uk/matador
Twitter: @matadorbooks

ISBN 978 1789015 584

British Library Cataloguing in Publication Data.
A catalogue record for this book is available from the British Library.

Typeset in 11pt Gill Sans by Troubador Publishing Ltd, Leicester, UK

Matador is an imprint of Troubador Publishing Ltd

For light lovers everywhere

CONTENTS

Introduction	ix
1. What is light?	1
2. A pyramid of light	5
3. The light-body connection	9
4. When we got wired	20
5. A light-compatible life	32
Image Credits	47

INTRODUCTION

Light – it's all around us. From the golden glow of the sun to the blue allure of the moon; from the enticing hot pink of a neon sign to the angry yellow flicker of a fluorescent tube. But do we ever stop to reflect on what light is and how it affects us? Is there a difference between the dazzling rays of summer sunshine and the bright white glare of an LED lamp?

This book is designed to get us thinking about light, help us learn a little about the different types of light we are exposed to, and provide simple tips on how to relate to them for maximum benefit.

This information is right on time, as awareness of the importance of light is growing. At the close of 2017, the Nobel Prize in Medicine was jointly awarded to Jeffrey C. Hall, Michael Rosbash and Michael W. Young for their discoveries of molecular mechanisms controlling *circadian rhythm* – the regular rhythm of the day that governs our biological clocks. Although scientists have long understood the link between light and circadian rhythm, the mechanisms behind it have been a 'black box' of mystery. With this Nobel Prize breakthrough, circadian research enters an exciting new era. UNESCO too has been raising awareness around light, choosing 16th May 2018 to launch its annual International Day of Light. This follows up from their 2015 initiative, the International Year of Light, which highlighted the importance of light-based sciences and technologies and saw participation from 147 countries.

With these societal milestones in mind, it's a good time to think about our personal relationship with light. Are we actively taking decisions about the kind of light we are exposed to, or do we simply take it for granted, without considering how lighting conditions can affect us? What might happen if we changed that dynamic?

I first started exploring my relationship with light in 2008, when I noticed I was becoming affected by winter depression. After making my lifestyle more light compatible and discovering the power of coloured light, I soon noticed dramatic improvements in my mood and performance. Now a coloured light therapist myself, it's a joy to see the same results in my clients.

I hope this book will contribute to raising awareness about the power of light and what we can do to optimise our relationship with it.

So, wherever you are in the world, whatever time of day it is, whether you're waking at dawn or winding down at dusk, join me and take a look at the light around us…

Candela Wicke

1
WHAT IS LIGHT?

For the rest of my life I will reflect on what light is
— Albert Einstein

As Einstein's comment suggests, the answer to our question is not as simple as it seems. In fact, it has puzzled humanity for centuries.

Ancient philosophers such as Euclid believed that our eyes possessed an inner fire, and that beams of light radiated from the pupils. When these burning jets hit external objects, they suddenly became visible. This idea may seem far-fetched to us now, but we still allude to the phenomena of someone having 'fiery eyes' or 'casting a glance' at something.

By the Mid-17th Century, Isaac Newton's experiments with glass prisms had prompted him to theorise that light consisted of microscopic coloured particles that bounced off surfaces, much like billiard balls bouncing off the cushions of a games table. As a keen billiards player, Newton found this a fitting image to describe the pathway of coloured light beams through a prism.

Nevertheless, Newton's notion was committed to the coffin in 1803, when optics genius Thomas Young demonstrated the wave-like behaviour of light with his double slit experiment. If light was a particle, then only the rays of light that exactly hit the slits could pass through, making a pattern of two straight lines (like the slits) on the screen behind them. But if light was a wave, its nature would cause the light passing through both slits to diffract and overlap, resulting in an interference pattern of bright and dark bands on the screen – a bit like butterfly wings. And this is what happened.

But the story did not end there. In fact, it was Einstein himself who resurrected the controversy in 1905, when he put two pieces of previous research together. In 1887, Heinrich Hertz had observed what is now known as the photoelectric effect: that ultraviolet light can cause electrons to be ejected from a metal surface. These results were puzzling, as they could not be explained by the accepted model of light behaving as wave. In 1900, Max Planck had suggested that light only existed in small packets or *quanta*. Perhaps this idea would literally shed light on the problem? In 1921, Einstein was awarded the Nobel Prize for advancing Planck's hypothesis to explain the photoelectric effect. However, it was another Nobel Prize winner, Louis De Broglie, who cemented the concept of wave-particle duality in 1929 and paved the way for our modern understanding of light as both particle and wave.

When light is a particle

When describing the impact of light on chemical processes, we like to talk about 'particles' of light energy, or *photons*. Just as an atom is the smallest particle of a material, so too the photon is the smallest particle of light. However, unlike material atoms, photons have no mass. They are electrically neutral and extremely stable. Photons of sufficient energy can interact with atoms, knocking their outer shell electrons into excited orbits and allowing them to participate in chemical reactions. One example is the production of Vitamin D in humans. When exposed to sunlight, a form of cholesterol in the skin absorbs high-energy photons, starting a series of reactions that makes Vitamin D3 available to the body. *Photobiology* – the study of light on living things – is an exciting and complex area of scientific research.

When light is a wave

Radio waves, microwaves… light can also be considered to be a wave. In fact, all three are forms of radiation, belonging to what is known as the electromagnetic spectrum. For most of human history, visible light was the only part we recognised. It wasn't until the 19th Century that scientists started to discover the spectrum's full scope and range, which extends far into the universe. Describing light as a wave is useful when we want to consider its reach, for example, how far it penetrates the skin. We measure wavelength in *nanometres* (nm). One nanometre is a billionth of a metre. Violet light has a relatively short wavelength (at approximately 400 nm) and will only penetrate the epidermis or upper layer of skin. On the other hand, infrared light (at approximately 700 nm) has a much longer wavelength and will penetrate deep down to the subcutaneous layer. These different wavelengths are employed in light therapies to treat various problems (more on this in Chapter 5).

THE ELECTROMAGNETIC SPECTRUM

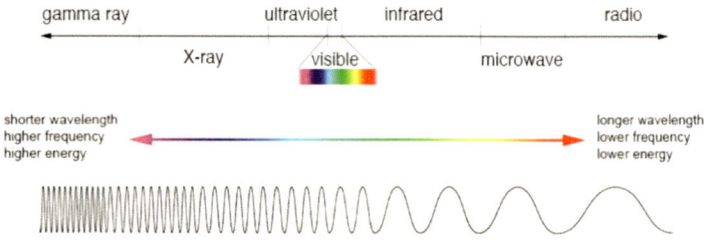

The visible spectrum or 'optical window' stretches from deep violet at 400 nm to dark red at 700 nm but the boundaries are subjective and approximate. Human vision reaches maximum sensitivity in the middle of this window at the lime-coloured wavelength of 550 nm. Sunlight contains the full spectrum of visible light as well as the adjoining infrared and ultraviolet radiation.

2
A PYRAMID OF LIGHT

The world is full of light. Natural light, electric light – what's the difference and is it important? We can start answering this question by considering the light around us as a pyramid of different components, just as we might consider food as a pyramid of different nutrients. Let's begin from the bottom and work our way up.

The first tier: natural light

The sun, moon and stars form our most basic sources of light – without them, life as we know it would not exist. The most important of these, *the Sun*, supplies enough photons to power every ecosystem on this planet. Environmentally friendly and absolutely free of charge, direct sunshine is the finest source of light. Exposure to sunlight is the only way we can feed our bodies the quantity and quality of light needed to fuel many biological functions.

Moonlight, although technically light reflected back from the sun, has a character of its own. Throughout human history, the Moon has been a source of irresistible fascination, spawning folklore, myths and legends. Under its power you can cast a spell or howl like a werewolf – the choice is yours. On a practical note, however, moonlight is strong enough for nocturnal navigation. In times past this was an asset to desert nomads, who preferred journeying in the cool of the night.

The stars too have fascinated us since time began. From navigating the seas to navigating space, they help us calculate our position in the universe.

As we can see from the pyramid, natural light forms the biggest tier. Just like protein in our food, it is an essential building block of life.

The second tier: firelight

Firelight was the first artificial form of light. Archaeological findings in South Africa date the intentional use of fire to around a million years ago. The miraculous flames were not only a light source that could instantly dispel darkness, but also a powerful protection from wild animals. It was the perfect weapon…

The radiation of naked flames has some important effects on our body rhythms. After a million years, we have been conditioned to interpret animated orange light as a ritual of the evening: a time for roast mammoth and rest. While prehistoric elephant is no longer on the menu, the amber glow of a fire still comforts us and triggers our brains into relaxation. Who can resist the delicious promise of a barbecue or the romance of an evening by candlelight?

Notice that firelight forms a very thin slice of the pyramid. These days, humans rarely rely on fire for illumination, although we still enjoy using it. This tier of light evokes the senses, a bit like aromatic spices in a delicious meal.

The third tier: electric light

Light at the flick of a switch is taken for granted now, but just imagine what an exotic oddity it was some hundred years ago. Hotels had to put up instruction signs to prevent innocent guests from trying to ignite the new Edison light bulb with matches. And at bedtime, confused visitors would still try to blow out the bulb like a candle. Fast-forward to the 21st Century and even the iconic light bulb has been rendered obsolete. Our world is lit up 24/7 with a dazzling array of fluorescents, halogens and LEDS.

Compared to the last two tiers, electric light is the shiny

new kid on the block. It's clean, instant and energy-efficient – no wonder we love it so much! However, the relative newness of electric light means we are only just starting to discover its impact on humans and other life forms. And some of these findings aren't pretty. Just like junk food, electric light should come with a health warning…

The fourth tier: the super lights

The twinkling peak of our pyramid takes us into the brave new world of lasers and other forms of coloured light: the super lights. You may already have heard about them or experienced their therapeutic effects. Quite rightly, this tier is tiny. The super lights are potent and only to be used in small doses. As concentrated pick-me-ups, they are like vitamin pills boosting a poor diet.

This is a simple overview, but as you can imagine, there's a lot to say about the different types of light. In fact, you could probably write an encyclopaedia about each one of them. Practicality prevents us here, however. So now that we've begun thinking about the different types of light, let's continue by looking at aspects that affect our everyday lives.

3
THE LIGHT-BODY CONNECTION

It may be stating the obvious: we all need light but have you stopped to consider why? These days, we think nothing of sharing our fitness and diet tips, but when was the last time you asked someone if they were getting enough light? The chances are they'd stare back at you blankly.

Light affects us on a physical and emotional level that we often feel intuitively but can rarely explain. We understand why plants lean towards the sun, but not why we do too. This is not surprising. It was not until 1984 that Dr Norman Rosenthal made the link between winter depression and lack of sunlight. And it took until 2017 before the Nobel Prize was awarded for lifting the lid on the mechanisms of our circadian rhythm. To answer why we need light, though, we need only to make some basic observations about our bodies and the environment.

Seeing is believing

It's a no-brainer: without light we cannot see. Try shutting your eyes – dark, isn't it? The human eye is a highly complex organ, but we can remind ourselves of its basic functions by taking a look at the diagram on the next page.

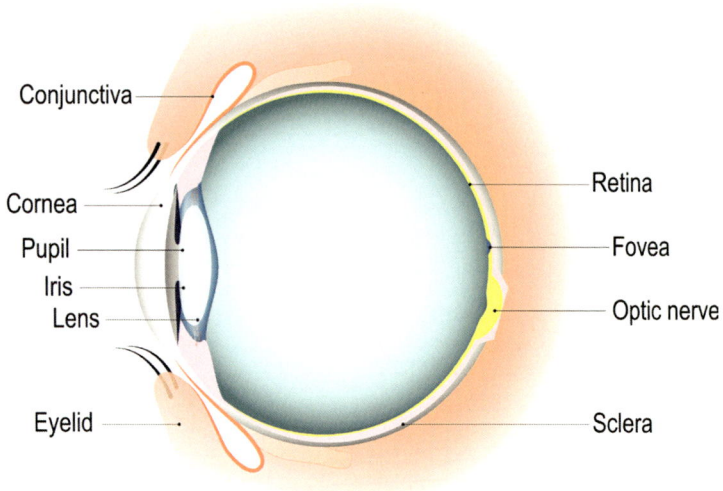

IRIS: The coloured part of the eye, the iris opens and closes to control the amount of light entering through the pupil. In dim light, the iris dilates as more light is allowed in. In bright light, the iris constricts to protect the eye from damage.

The PUPIL is the dark hole in the middle of the iris where light enters.

CORNEA: This transparent outer layer at the front of the eye is responsible for about 70% of its focusing power.

LENS: Changes shape to focus light on the retina. The lens is responsible for about 30% of the eye's focusing power.

RETINA: This contains three types of light receptor cells: rods, cones and ganglion cells. The rods work at very low levels of light to give us grey-scale night vision, while the cones require high levels of light to enable sharp focus and colour vision. The photosensitive ganglion cells are neurons, transmitting information to the brain over time, thereby helping to regulate our circadian rhythm.

FOVEA: At the centre of the retina is a tiny pit containing the highest concentration of cones and providing the sharpest vision. Its position directly on the focal point of the lens makes it highly vulnerable to piercing light of high frequency. It is naturally protected by a shielding yellow filter called the macula lutea.

So our eyes are finely tuned to adapt to different levels of light. As youngsters, we often take it for granted but as we get older we become increasingly aware of this function – or the lack of it. A sixty-year-old, for example, needs three times more light than a twenty-year-old for the same visual performance. This is because as we age, the muscles that control our pupil size lose strength, making the pupils smaller and less responsive to changes in ambient lighting. Vision is not the only bodily function dependent on light entering the eyes, however.

Tick-tock, everybody's on the clock

The physiological processes of living things – plants, animals, humans, bacteria – are all approximately tuned to day and night cycles. This is what we are referring to when we talk about our *circadian rhythm* or body clock. One example of a process it governs is the human sleep/wake cycle. When it gets dark, our eyes signal to the brain that it's time to sleep. When it gets light, the reverse happens. Of course, that is extremely simplistic. There are dozens of complex mechanisms involved, from light-sensitive protein responses in the retina to hormonal release in the hypothalamus. And these processes are driven, not by one single clock chiming out the hour, but by a vast network of inter-related cellular clocks. So what we perceive to be one cycle is in fact an intricate interplay of many. Our circadian rhythms can also vary slightly from individual to individual. Are you a night owl or lark, old or young?

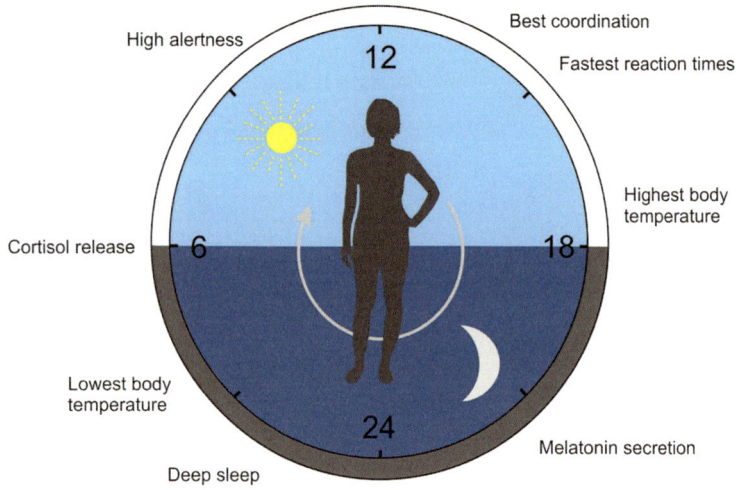

A selection of physiological responses governed by our circadian rhythm

Midsummer madness or Midwinter grumps?

Our relationship with light also becomes apparent with the change of seasons. For people living in the Northern hemisphere, this can bring noticeable fluctuations in light levels. In the autumn we frown and mutter about the nights 'drawing in'; in the spring we step out into the lighter evenings with a smile on our faces. Such seasonal differences are most extreme at higher latitudes and can be profoundly disturbing. In summer, people overdose on natural light 24/7, with hyperactivity and sleep deprivation taking its toll. In winter, the reverse is true – the lack of light sapping energy levels and fuelling mood disorders.

But seasonal variations are natural, so why can it be difficult to cope with them? Our sensitivity to light is rooted in our evolutionary beginnings. Early humans emerged from the equatorial savannas of Africa, where days and nights were of roughly equal length all year round. These stable conditions became the temporal standard for our body clocks. Although migration would force adaptation to more extreme variations in light and darkness, a preference for equatorial balance has remained deep within us.

When things get out of synch

When we really notice our connection to light, however, is when things get out of synch. Flying from Los Angeles to London? Hello jet lag! Travelling across several time zones can seriously disrupt our body clocks. We may find ourselves instantly falling asleep at noon or feeling wide awake at midnight. Why? Our body clocks are anticipating the rising and setting of the sun in the old time zone rather than simply reacting to the new one.

Shift workers experience a similar problem. They have had to train themselves to stay alert and work during the hours the body is normally least energetic. If subjected to this anomaly long term, serious health issues may result. Memory and ability to focus can become impaired; irritability or depression may be additional side-effects. These symptoms have been widely recognised as shift-work sleep disorder and many 24-hour organisations are re-thinking their schedules to reduce its impact.

> ### Did you know?
>
> If the brain is suffering from light starvation, it will react by over-producing the sleep hormone melatonin. Common symptoms are fatigue and confusion often occurring in combination with a craving for fast carbs. Conversely, an overdose of light disrupts melatonin production, with adverse effects on bodily repair processes that rely on darkness. Long-term disruption can cause the internal body clock to become permanently disturbed, increasing susceptibility to chronic diseases.

Light starvation you say? While nature sometimes starves us of precious daylight, mostly it is our own fault we go hungry. And we don't have to be jet-setters or shift-workers to suffer. We started out as outdoor animals, adapted to fresh air and sunlight but our recently adopted, comfortable lifestyles have interfered with that. Most of us are urbanites, living and working indoors. We shut the shutters and draw the curtains, preferring the light of a computer screen to the light outside.

Ironically, people living with plentiful sunshine all year round can be most at risk of light starvation. Sheltering from the glare and heat of the sun in air-conditioned buildings from morning till night means constant light deprivation, leading to serious Vitamin D deficiency and related disease. The Middle East and Africa, for instance, have the highest levels of rickets and osteoporosis in the world.

> ....
> ### Ask yourself:
> ....
>
> How long have I spent outside today?
>
> Most of us spend some 90% of our lives indoors with limited access to full daylight. That translates as 2.4 hours per day. Do the maths – did you even manage that? You're not the only one.

Eat light

So now the light-body connection is clear: we need natural light to function properly. Unfortunately, our geographic location and lifestyle can make things difficult and light starvation is a real risk. What can we do about it? Luckily, a few simple changes to our habits can work wonders. Just like eating the right foods, 'eating' the right light can drastically improve our wellbeing. Our individual circumstances will affect the way we go about it, however. Let us look at a couple of scenarios.

The London office worker

Eighty-percent of the year, the skies are grey. Bright sunshine is an occasional treat, not an everyday delight. In the morning you leave your dingy apartment for the cramped confines of public transport and spend the day glued to your desk in an artificially lit office. It is not uncommon for you to arrive home in darkness, after drowning your sorrows in an equally dark pub.

Clearly, this person needs to get outside more. If climate

and working conditions are an obstacle, you're going to have to make an effort. Walk or cycle to work if you can. Open the blinds in the office and sit by the window. Take breaks outside during the brightest hours of the day, especially in winter. Consistently increasing your intake of natural light – even on an overcast day – can have a positive effect on energy level and mood.

The Australian airline pilot

Every day's a blue sky day – both up in the air and down on the ground. The sun shines as a rule, not an exception. In fact, this person has to be more careful than most about exposure to UV radiation. Sitting in the cockpit above the clouds for an hour is said to be equivalent to 20 minutes on a sunbed. And when you're at home on the ground in sunny Australia, those solar rays will be relentless.

But does that mean avoiding sunlight at all cost? No. Going for a walk in broad daylight is the best way to help cure your jet lag. Choose early morning or evening to avoid the harshest rays. When you're flying, use a biodegradable sunscreen on your face and hands; when you're on the ground, dial up the protection by seeking shade. Regularly exposing other parts of your body to gentle sunlight for brief periods will help maintain levels of Vitamin D.

These may be two extreme examples but they get us thinking about our own circumstances and habits in relation to the light around us. Am I spending enough time in natural light? And what about electric light? Surely good quality light indoors can compensate for the lack of it outdoors? The following chapters will help answer these questions.

Who's afraid of the sun?

Almost everybody these days. Decades of being warned about the dangerous effects of UV radiation has meant many people slap on sunscreen day in, day out, whatever the weather. But persistently preventing our skin from absorbing light can be far more dangerous. Without sunlight we cannot naturally synthesise Vitamin D, and we need to expose at least 10% of our body area to do that. Twenty minutes of unprotected exposure to the sun, 2-4 times a week is good practice to maintain adequate levels, although this is only a basic guideline. How much light is needed will vary with the individual – the darker your skin, the more sunlight you will need. And simply exposing your face and hands is not what is meant here – these parts generally get plenty of light. Instead, try to expose parts you normally cover up: your stomach, legs and feet, for example. When possible, nude sunbathing also has many advantages. Sunlight on the pelvic region is particularly beneficial, as it fortifies the bones and boosts the health of the reproductive organs in both men and women.

Photosensitivity – be aware

Although sun exposure has multiple benefits, it should be approached with caution. If you are fair-skinned, blond or a red-head, you should generally seek shade, cover up with loose clothes and use biodegradable sunscreens. Some people have medical conditions that make them particularly sensitive to sunlight. Others take medications or have contact with chemicals that can cause sensitivity. Here are some examples. If in doubt, consult your doctor.

- Sulfa used in some drugs, among them some antibiotics, diuretics, COX-2 inhibitors, and diabetes drugs.
- Psoralens, coal tars, photo-active dyes (eosin, acridine orange)
- Musk ambrette, methylcoumarin, lemon oil (may be present in fragrances)
- PABA (found in some chemical sunscreens)
- Oxybenzone (UVA and UVB chemical blocker in some chemical sunscreens)
- Salicylanilide (found in industrial cleaners)
- St John's Wort – used to treat depression
- Hexachlorophene (found in some antibacterial soaps)
- Contact with sap from Giant Hogweed. Common Rue is another phototoxic plant commonly found in gardens.
- Tetracycline antibiotics

Did you know?

It's not just an old wives' tale: sunlight is a great disinfectant. And that's one reason your grandmother probably preferred to hang the washing out in the sun rather than throw it in the tumble drier. In recent times, the use of ultraviolet light (the disinfecting portion of sunlight) has been revived, for example, in the purification of drinking water or swimming pools. UV disinfection leaves water clean and fresh, with none of the irritating side-effects of chemical treatments.

For more information on the power of sunlight go to
www.sunlightinstitute.org

4
WHEN WE GOT WIRED

Ever since Edison invented the tungsten light bulb, the world has been in love with electric light. No longer would we have to put up with the sooty fumes of kerosene lamps, or live with the explosive danger of gaslights. Clean light came by flicking a switch, not by fumbling for a match.

Electric lighting rapidly proved itself a boon to society. Increased illumination made streets feel safer and round-the-clock travel suddenly became feasible. In factories, work could continue far into the night, increasing production and reducing lead times. After just a few decades, a taste for industrialisation and urbanisation would cause the world to crave electric light in huge amounts. But are we starting to feel any ill effects?

Electric light ≠ daylight

Intuitively, we know electric light is different to natural light but how do we explain it? Quite simply, electric light does not have the same ingredients as sunlight or has them in the wrong proportions. As mentioned in the previous chapter, sunlight feeds our biological systems and electric light simply cannot substitute – it would be like eating paraffin instead of butter. So consuming large amounts of artificial light is going to give us an almighty attack of indigestion. But understanding the difference between electric light and natural light is not as easy as understanding the difference between paraffin and butter. An analysis of ingredients will make things clear, however.

What the spectrum reveals

The spectrum of a light source is the profile or 'fingerprint' of the wavelengths of light it emits. Below we can compare the spectrum of sunlight with that of different types of electric light.

Sunlight

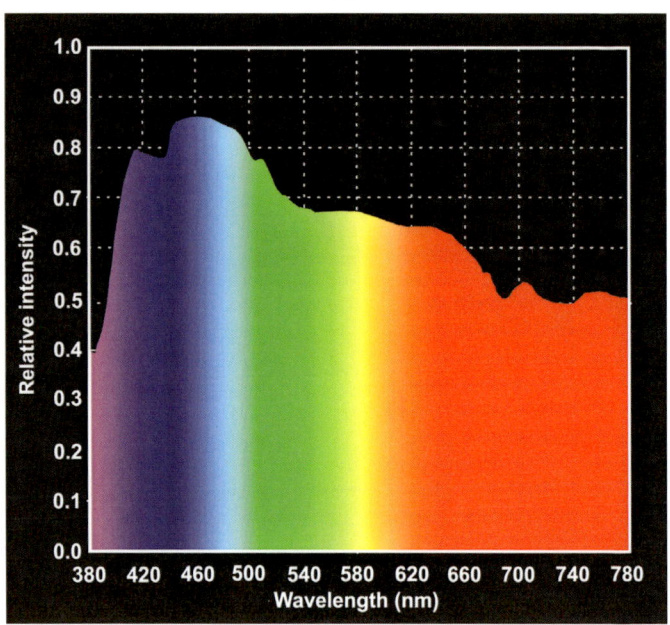

Incandescent

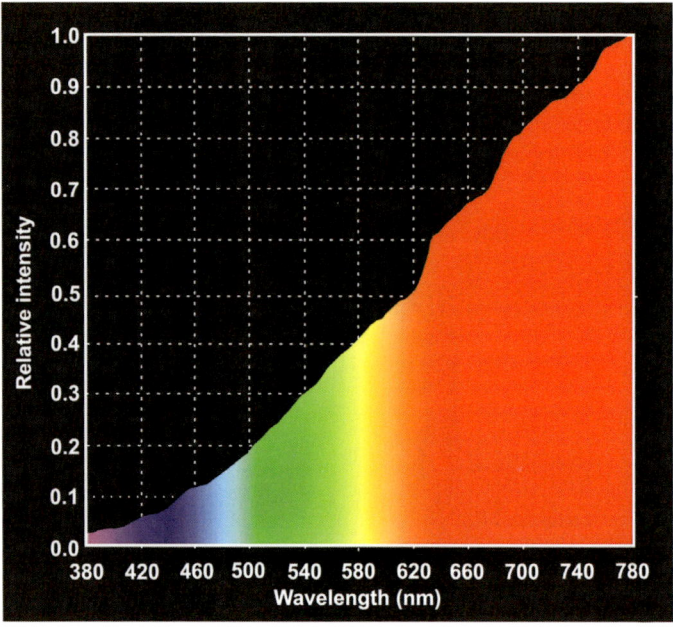

Halogen

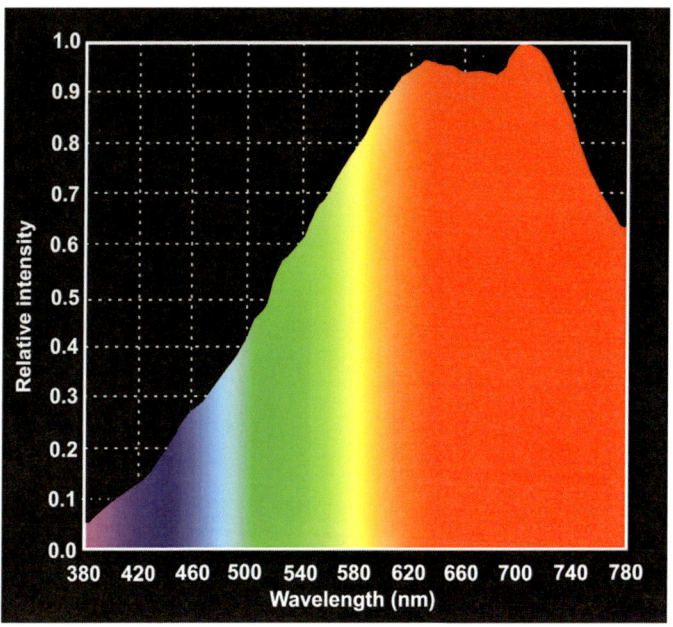

Fluorescent

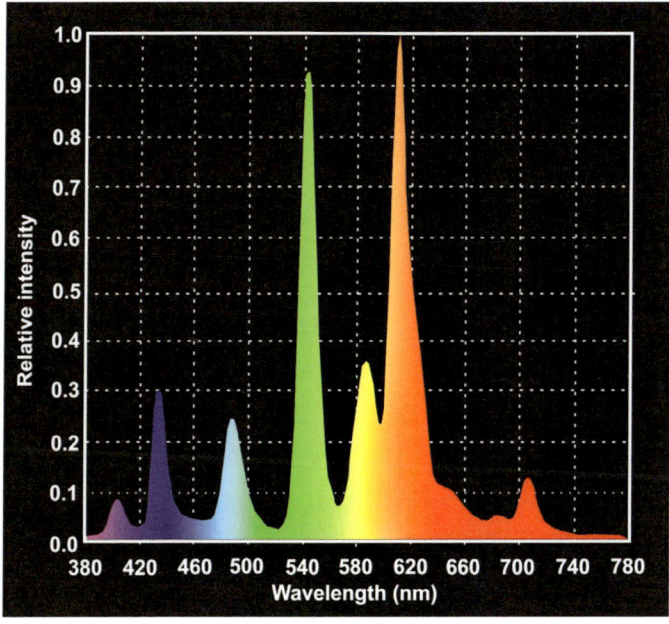

LED

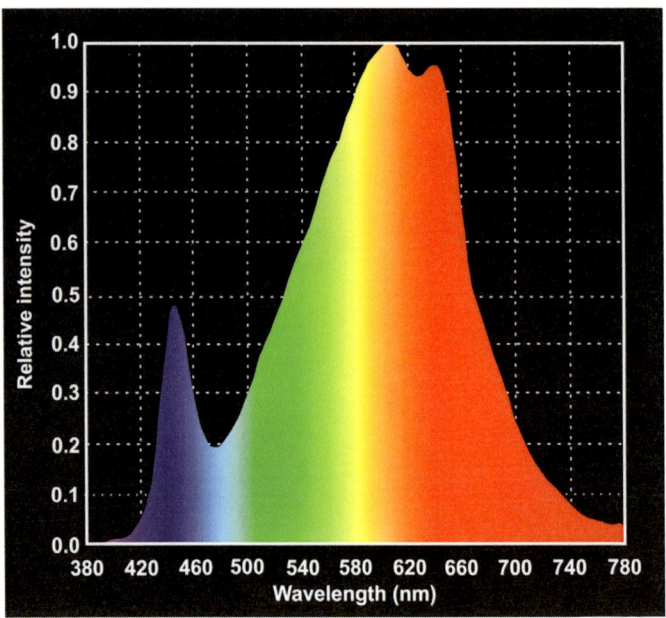

OLED

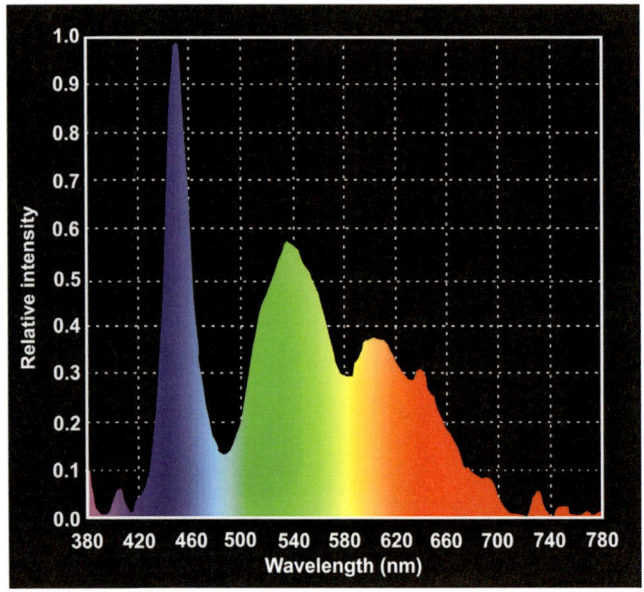

Sunlight

The full spectrum of daylight in all its glory: relatively high intensities of all the wavelengths in the visible spectrum, with a large proportion of red but softly peaking in the blue. Full spectrum means it contains all the components of light our bodies need and feel most comfortable with. For example, UVB at around 300 nm helps us synthesise vitamin D, while infrared at approximately 700 nm is warming and penetrates deep into the tissues, improving microcirculation.

Incandescent

If a light source is incandescent, it generates heat. Humans have a long relationship with this type of warm light, as all early light sources – fire, candles, kerosene – were incandescent. A modern example of an incandescent is the traditional tungsten light bulb, the spectrum of which we see here. The curve is quite smooth, but compared to natural daylight, it is far more intense in the red to infrared and almost entirely lacking in the blue. Due to excessive heat output and poor energy efficiency, the traditional light bulb has been widely banned or phased out worldwide.

Halogen

This is also an incandescent light source, but more energy efficient than a traditional bulb. Notice that of all the spectrums, halogen's is the most like that of natural daylight. The white light of halogens is ideal for visually demanding precision work and its good colour rendering properties make it a popular choice for window displays. Fed by direct current, a halogen light never pulsates or flickers, so eye strain is reduced. Standard halogen bulbs do get very hot though, and this is one reason cooler LEDs now dominate the market. However, more energy-efficient types of halogen lighting are being developed all the time and these may well become the preferred light source in the future.

Fluorescent   Compact Fluorescent

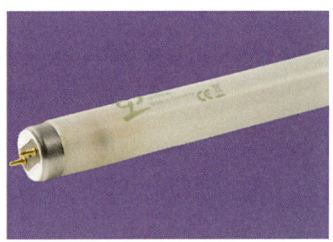 

This type of lighting lurks about in factories, offices and old bathrooms, making everyone look ill. And it can literally make you feel ill too. As you can see, the spectrum is very jagged with sharp peaks, quite unlike natural light. The mercury in fluorescents is a health hazard and the irritation of constant flicker is reason enough for a headache… Safer alternatives to standard fluorescents are now available but the quality of their light is still a far cry from natural light or incandescent sources.

A special note about CFLs (compact fluorescents) also known as energy-saving light bulbs

In the Mid 1990s, before LED lighting became mainstream, CFL s were heavily pushed as an energy-saving alternative to conventional light bulbs. While the switch saved households energy, it did nothing to improve the lighting environment. These light sources are simply mini versions of their fluorescent tube cousins, with exactly the same unnatural spectrum. Due to their small size and compatibility with standard light fittings, many people only know them as energy-saving light bulbs and do not even realise they are fluorescents.

LED

In an attempt to curb energy wastage, the world has gone mad for LEDs. These lights produce a lot less heat than incandescents and have incredibly long lives but what about the quality of their light? The spectrum shows sharp peaks and troughs where natural daylight has none. This is problematic. The concentration of blue will make this light too harsh for the home and overexposure in the evenings can upset our circadian rhythms and disrupt sleep.

OLED

The demand for LED lighting has presented some issues in terms of sourcing and recycling rare earth metals and other components. This is one area in which OLEDs have an advantage, as they utilise an organic compound as a semiconductor rather than a metal one. OLEDs also have some picture rendering qualities which may make them more desirable than LEDs in screen technology, although the expense currently limits their use to high end TVs and mobile phones. Looking back at the spectrum, we see jagged peaks and troughs, as for LEDs, and an even higher peak in the blue.

Blue in the Face

Did you know that staring at your flat screen TV, laptop, tablet or mobile phone = staring at an LED/OLED and exposing yourself to excessive blue radiation? The screens of all of these devices have spectra similar to the example of the OLED mobile phone above, with a sharp peak in blue. We wouldn't dream of gazing endlessly at a ceiling light, but we think nothing of gazing at our iPads for hours. The fact that we constantly look at these screens – for work and pleasure – means the cells of our retinas are under persistent stress from high intensity blue radiation. Apart from disrupting our sleep patterns, excessive exposure to the light from these devices may also lead to age-related macular degeneration (AMD), which is an incurable condition that can gradually lead to blindness. See page 36 for advice on how to minimise your exposure to harmful blue light.

V is for Volume

It's obvious when you think about it but so easy to forget: the volume of incoming natural light from the sky is huge. Electric lighting is no match for the sun. To illustrate: the EU recommends 500 lux (see below) as adequate illumination for an office. Many indoor environments provide much less. But a sunny Florida beach with reflecting white sands and glittering waters will easily provide an impressive 150 000 lux. It's not hard to guess where we'd feel happiest.

> ## How do we measure light?
>
> We can measure light intensity in terms of lux and lumens. One lux roughly compares to the illumination provided by a full moon. By comparison, on a clear day, ambient outdoor light is about 400 lux. Sunlight ranges from 32 000 to 100 000 lux. How much light do we need for various activities? Some current standard recommendations are:
>
> - 100 lux in a living room
> - 500 lux in office areas
> - 1000 lux for precision work
>
> When lighting a space, we consider lumens. A lumen is a standardised unit of measurement for the total amount of light produced by a light source, such as a lamp. One lux is defined as being equivalent to one lumen spread over an area of one square metre.

So now we're getting the picture. Electric light simply isn't the same as daylight. And the differences we've highlighted demonstrate that in some ways, our electric buddy isn't our best friend. In fact, he could be our worst enemy. Let's see why.

There's something about ALAN

Who on earth is ALAN? Well, he's a baddie, gradually killing natural darkness by flooding the night with unnecessary light pollution. ALAN, or Artificial Light at Night, encompasses everything from humble street signs to giant electronic billboards, floodlights on your driveway to the trail of headlights on a freeway.

Greenhouses, airports and sports arenas are some of ALAN's most lethal weapons, their polluting light radiating in all possible directions and drowning organic patterns of light. The light-smog wipes out detailed vision, firstly via the direct effects of faulty illumination and then via the indirect sky glow. Astronomers are finding it increasingly difficult to locate areas of sufficient darkness for their telescopes to make accurate observations of the night sky.

This loss of natural darkness is not just a nuisance to astronomers, it is causing serious harm to the environment. Nocturnal animals in particular suffer from disorientation. Migrating birds, sea turtle hatchlings and insects are similarly affected by light pollution. Humans are not immune either. We need the strong luminous contrast between broad daylight and deep darkness to stabilise our body clocks and keep our eyes healthy. Excessive exposure to ALAN (particularly blue light) can impair our night vision and has been linked to increased risk of depression, diabetes, obesity and other serious disorders.

"Many species (including humans) need darkness to survive and thrive."

American Medical Association Council on Science and Public Health (2012)

So what can we do?

ALAN-induced insomnia, fluorescent-triggered migraine, poor night vision… yes, the ill effects of electric light are real. Our overconsumption is giving us indigestion. But are we just going to lie down and clutch at our sore stomachs, or can we change our light-eating habits for the sake of our health and that of the environment? The answer is: YES, WE CAN!

The next chapter will guide us through practical things we can do to optimise our relationship with all types of light. It also contains links to websites where you can find more advice and tips on specific areas.

Pretty or pretty dim? The bright lights of Shanghai with accompanying light smog

5

A LIGHT-COMPATIBLE LIFE

Having considered the light-body connection and what happened when we got wired, it's time to see how we can live a light-compatible life. But let's be realistic. We're not going to abandon the comfort of our houses for a nomadic existence on the steppes and we won't be swapping our electric light bulbs for flaming torches any time soon. There are much simpler ways to let more of the right kind of light into our lives. Let's take a look.

Max out on natural light

Remembering our London office worker and Australian airline pilot from Chapter 3, you're probably thinking this involves getting outdoors more. Well you'd be right, but we can do a number of other things to max out on natural light.

1. Open up

Are there shutters, blinds or curtains in your home or place of work? Open them up and let the light in! Obviously there are times when these light inhibitors are necessary but if you are spending all day indoors you need exposure to as much natural light as much as possible. This is of special importance to city dwellers, for whom natural light is already limited due to the lack of space between buildings.

2. Ditch the black

You might think it sophisticated or practical, but wearing black all the time permanently shuts out light from your body. If you are pregnant, it's even worse, as no light can reach your growing foetus. Choose light-coloured clothing as much as possible and remember to expose different areas of bare skin to sunlight for twenty minutes, 2-4 times a week, to safeguard against Vitamin D deficiency and osteoporosis.

3. Avoid hoods, scarves, hats and sunglasses

Likewise, constantly covering your head with hoods, scarves and hats or wearing sunglasses at the slightest hint of sunshine will deprive your body of much needed light. Light enters the body through the cranium as well as the eyes, directly influencing brain function. Hoods and sunglasses may sometimes be necessary but simply wearing them to look cool will do your head no favours.

> *–A dark house is always an unhealthy house –*
> *Florence Nightingale*

Embrace natural darkness

As highlighted in Chapter 4, ALAN is robbing us of natural darkness, and we have to put up a fight for our health and the environment! What simple steps can we take?

1. Block it out

When you switch all the lights off at bedtime, take a look around you. Is your bedroom completely dark or can you spot any light bugs? As your eyes adjust to the darkness, it may take a minute or so to notice them. Perhaps a thin stream of light from the street is beating down on your pillow through a pair of ill-fitting curtains. What about the coloured diodes on your electrical devices, or the green glare of an air-conditioning control panel? Is your mobile phone screen constantly flashing with notifications? These sources of ALAN often go unnoticed until everything else is switched off.

Outside sources of ALAN can be eliminated with well-fitting black-out blinds or curtains. Inside sources simply need to be switched off. But if pulling the plug on a device isn't an option, try taping over or covering the light temporarily with something opaque. In hotel rooms, for example, black socks come in very useful for this! Alternatively, invest in a comfortable sleeping mask to carry when you travel. That way you will always have an instant black-out solution, ensuring your retinas can recharge overnight in total darkness.

2. Join the Dark Sky movement

The International Dark Sky Association was founded in 1988 with the aim of protecting our night skies for present and future generations. Their work involves educating the public and policy makers about night sky conservation and promoting environmentally responsible outdoor lighting. You can become a member and get involved in many of their awareness-raising initiatives, for example, International Dark Sky Week in April each year. For more information go to www.darksky.org

3. Camp in the wilderness

If you live in an urban area, your eyes and brain will greatly benefit from escaping those city lights from time to time. If possible, retreat to a national park for the weekend and go camping. Unlike ALAN, starlight is far too distant and weak to disrupt our night time rhythms. Sleeping under the velvet canopy of a naturally dark sky is a blissful experience that will leave the rod cells in your retinas recharged and refreshed. Periods of contrast between light and dark are necessary for the optimal functioning of the eye.

How bad is ALAN where I live?

Go to **www.cires.colorado.edu/Artificial-light** to find out. The New World Atlas of Artificial Sky Brightness is most enlightening!

Get screen savvy

Whether we like it or not, using computers, tablets and smart phones has become essential to modern life. We work with them all day and play with them all evening. But this exposure is wreaking havoc with our eye health. The fovea, near the centre of the retina, is particularly sensitive to the high frequency blue radiation that comes from these screens. With excessive bombardment, the macula lutea – a yellowish layer that protects the fovea – can become damaged, seriously impairing all central vision, particularly colour vision. We all need to protect ourselves from this, for the health of our eyes now and later in old age. How?

1. Use a colour temperature adjustment app

You can use an app to adapt your screen to cut out blue radiation in the evening. For example, try downloading F.lux for your computer, Lux for Android devices or use the pre-installed Night Shift setting from sunset to sunrise on your Apple device (iOS 9.3 and above).

2. Limit your kids' screen time

Protect your child's vision by being cruel to be kind – limit their use of tablets and computers during the day and ban them in the evening. They will complain it's unfair but may thank you later for saving their vision. And you can be an example by banning yourself from screen time too!

3. Wear yellow glasses when using your devices

Apart from minimising screen time, an effective way of

cutting out blue radiation is to wear yellow/amber glasses when using your devices. Go to www.innovative-eyewear.com for more information on coloured lens glasses and eye health.

Be fussy about electric lighting

In Chapter 4 we saw how different types of electric light can differ vastly to natural light and have a negative impact on our wellbeing and the environment. We can minimise these ill effects by choosing our electric lighting carefully. How should we go about it?

1. Avoid the F word

In this case, F is for fluorescents – and that includes modern compact fluorescents (CFL). The jagged spectrum and flicker of these light sources is highly irritating to our eyes and brain and the mercury vapour they contain is a biological hazard. If you have a tendency to suffer from migraine, vertigo or chronic fatigue, avoid fluorescent lighting as far as possible. This can be difficult, however. The energy efficiency and cheapness of fluorescents make them a popular choice for large public spaces such as offices and gyms. You may have to start a campaign in your workplace or community to implement change.

2. Pick and choose your LEDs/OLEDS

LED lighting is pretty much everywhere, but you can reduce the amount of blue radiation you are exposed to by fitting a warm white bulb rather than a cool white one. Colour temperature is also important. The higher the colour temperature of a light source, the more high-energy blue radiation it will emit. Choose a bulb with a colour temperature of 3 000 Kelvin or below, as these will be kinder to your eyes. If you can't see the information you need on the packaging, ask! Can the vendor show you the spectrum of the light source you are considering? This will really help you navigate the jungle of LED lighting products, some of which even claim to replicate daylight or look like a traditional filament light bulb. The spectrum will reveal just how healthy the light source is. Turn back to page 22-24 to refresh your memory of what you should be looking for.

Another source of unhealthy LED light exposure is flashing fairy lights and other twinkly trinkets. The market is awash with cheap decorative lights and toys, not to mention a plethora of laser pointers and other gadgets that use coloured LEDs. Apart from contributing to ALAN, use of these non-essential devices can seriously impair the health of your eyes. Sorry kids! Be particularly wary of devices emitting blue light, as the high-energy radiation can damage your retina.

3. Opt for Halogen and look out for developments in energy-efficient incandescents

As mentioned in Chapter 4, halogen is the best quality light available. Its colour rendering index (CRI) is a full 100 – compared to LED sources, which rarely exceed 90. For a number of years, halogen lighting has been condemned for producing a lot of heat and being far less energy-efficient than LED sources. But the new generation of energy-saving halogens is much more efficient and eco-friendly, making them the most natural alternative to the traditional incandescent light bulb. Growing awareness of the advantages of incandescent light has also coincided with some exciting research from institutes such as MIT that could see the traditional light bulb return in a form that is even more energy-efficient than LEDs. Keep a look out for new product developments!

The world of electric lighting is vast and complex, with market competitors all vying for consumer attention. The information they provide about various types of lighting is sometimes confusing and misleading. But by following the three guidelines above, you can start making healthier choices about the electric light you are exposed to.

Play safe with fire

So far, not much has been said about fire light. Looking back at page 5, we see it is only a narrow tier of the light pyramid. In modern life, we have little patience with sooty flames indoors or out. But while we understand the health hazards and impracticality of using fire, our biological affinity with this light source still draws us to its comforting glow. And there is one type of fire light that seems to keep us all enthralled and shopkeepers happy: candles. Yes, candles are big business.

In recent years, the trend for highly sophisticated scented candles has burgeoned. We all love a posh candle for Christmas! But we should not forget the dangers. All candles rob the atmosphere of oxygen and emit fumes, particularly if they are infused with fragrance. Paraffin wax candles are the worst, as they release toxic chemicals like benzene and toluene and a great deal of soot. If you want to use a candle occasionally, keep the room well ventilated and use a natural (e.g. beeswax or soy) candle containing only natural fragrances. These burn more slowly, do not release soot, and are made from sustainable resources.

Sup on the super lights

At the very pinnacle of the pyramid, we have a tiny and exclusive tier: the super lights. What are they and why are they so super?

You may recall from our discussion about the nature of light in Chapter 1 that we can split white light into its constituent colours, corresponding to different wavelengths. This concentrated monochromatic (pure coloured) light has specific effects that we have learned to harness. Let's take a look at the widest applications.

Red/Infrared

Red light in the range 600 - 1 350 nm (which includes infrared) has the ability to penetrate the skin deep into the subcutaneous tissue, where it activates the mitochondria in the cells to repair damage and promote healing. Infrared also improves microcirculation, increasing the flow of nutrients and oxygen and allowing more efficient elimination of toxins. Having recognised these effects, we can put them to good use. NASA, for example, was an early adopter, using infrared diodes to maintain muscle and joint health in astronauts. But now that infrared technology has moved on and is more widely available, we increasingly see it in:

- **Sports medicine** – for the relief of cramps, inflammation and sprains, and to improve conditions such as tennis elbow

- **Skin care** – for treating acne, scars, fine lines and to boost collagen production
- **Hair loss management** – to promote microcirculation in the scalp, stimulating hair growth

These treatments were previously only offered by professionals, but now many red and infrared devices are available for home use, include red light face treatment masks, infrared brushes/combs/caps for scalp health and infrared wands/wraps for muscle and joint pain.

Blue

We have mentioned avoiding blue light at night due to its overstimulating effects and potential to damage the eyes, but light in the wavelength range 495-415 nm (seen as blue) has potent super qualities. At the shorter end of blue near the violet (400-415 nm) the effects are antibacterial but with little penetration of the skin. At the longer end of the blue range (450-490 nm) there is deeper penetration of the skin with less antibacterial action. But these longer wavelengths of blue light can interact with the blood in the capillaries, neutralizing toxins as they pass through. Different wavelengths of blue light therefore have a range of medical uses, for example:

- **To kill bacteria and viruses** – such as the bacteria associated with acne or the nasty hospital bug MRSA
- **To neutralize blood toxins** – such as those caused by neonatal jaundice and other liver disorders which result in failure to break down the metabolic waste product bilirubin
- **To treat psoriasis** – blue light reduces inflammation and

regulates skin cell production but has none of the skin-damaging effects of ultraviolet light, which used to be a more common treatment for psoriasis

Just like infrared, blue light therapy is now more widely available for personal use. The most common applications include small wearable devices for acne or psoriasis treatment, portable light boxes for the treatment of SAD, and oral devices for gum health and tooth whitening. It is important to note that you should shield your eyes from direct exposure to the blue light when using these devices.

Seeing the rainbow

There are other ways to benefit from the super lights, and not always for a specific ailment or concern. They may be used to help improve mood and cognitive performance or simply enhance wellbeing on an abstract level. Many therapies work with the whole rainbow of colours. The results differ according to the type of light used, its intensity and how it is projected. Here are some examples:

- **Syntonics** The patient sits in a dark room and looks at a circle of coloured light. It is used to treat visual problems such as strabismus (cross eyes) and is particularly successful in head injury patients. The colour of the light used is decided by the type of visual problem. Developed by H. Riley Spitler as far back as the 1920s, syntonic phototherapy is popular with American optometrists.
- **Sensora and SensoSphere** The Sensora provides a multi-sensorial environment. Subjects are seated on a reclining armchair and view coloured light projected on to a large circular screen. A special audio track is played, with the

sound converted into kinaesthetic sensations in the armchair. Derived from the Sensora, the SensoSphere is a portable mood light. The beautiful orb can generate single colours or combinations to promote relaxation, balance or energy, as the user wishes. Both systems can be very useful on an emotional level and for alleviating symptoms of PTSD, anxiety, depression or SAD, to name a few.

- **Monocrom light dome and mask** Exceptionally pure coloured light is projected into a dome lowered over the head, or a mask worn over the eyes. The user can glide seamlessly from one end of the spectrum to the other, and is in complete control of what colours they choose to view. A course of three ten-minute treatments, three weeks apart can greatly enhance mood, focus and cognitive performance, as well as help alleviate conditions such as anxiety or SAD.

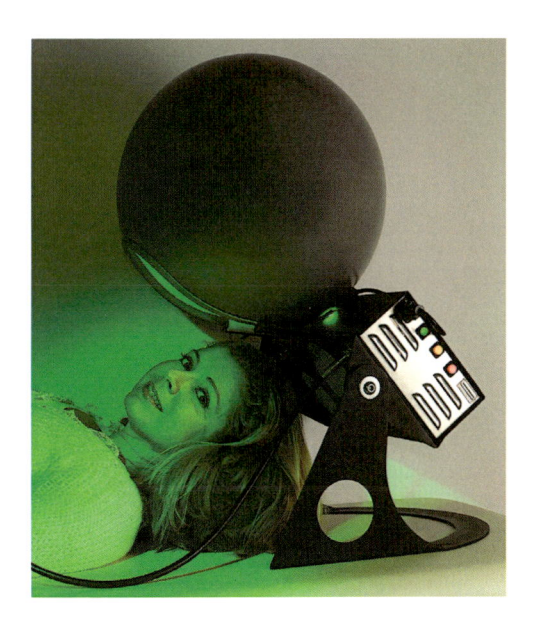

These are just three examples of how light and colour are used to improve wellbeing but there are many more. Which ones you try is up to you – our perceptions and preferences are unique to us and cannot be dictated. The important thing is to be open to the experience. Let light and colour into your life and observe the effects. You may be pleasantly surprised by the results!

START NOW

So there we have it: the power of light in a nut shell. Or in our case, a pyramid. From the most fundamental tier of natural light to the sparkling peak of the super lights, we have seen what the different types of light can do. But what will we do? Will we take action and change our light-eating habits – munching on natural light as much as possible, cutting out junk light and boosting our health with the super lights? Or will we simply gobble up whatever scraps the man-made environment throws at us?

I hope you have been inspired to try a light-compatible lifestyle. If you care about your health and the environment, start now – there's no time like the present. Do a little audit of the lighting conditions in your home. Can you change the light bulbs or the curtains? What about at work? Perhaps you can encourage your colleagues to take their lunch break with you outside. Ask your employer to consider bringing in a light therapist, particularly in the winter months. Many companies offer physiotherapy or massage – why not light treatments?

Small efforts can go a long way to helping us get the best from the light around us. And with wellbeing so clearly linked to light, shouldn't that be a priority? After all, as Marilyn Monroe once said:

We are all of stars, and we deserve to twinkle

IMAGE CREDITS

1. Cover illustration: USA at night, NASA composite satellite image, 2012
2. Sun over water, Donald34, iStock photo
3. Electromagnetic spectrum, NASA Imagine the universe
4. Light pyramid, Laszlo Incze
5. Eye diagram, iStock photo
6. Sunlight, iStock photo
7. Circadian Rhythm, Alan Hart
8. Hong Kong by night, Alan Hart
9. Shanghai light smog, Alan Hart
10-15 Light source spectra, Kjell Wallin
16. Sunlight, iStock photo
17-21 Light sources, Laszlo Incze
22. Monocrom light dome, Laszlo Incze
23. Pinwheel Galaxy (M101), NASA

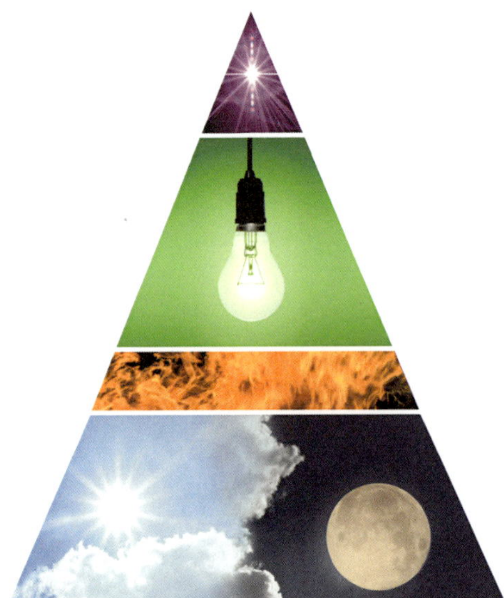